# SIZES IN GOD'S WORLD

written by
# Beverly Beckmann

illustrated by
# Jules Edler

CONCORDIA®
Publishing House
St. Louis

Copyright © 1984 Concordia Publishing House
3558 S. Jefferson Avenue, St. Louis, MO 63118-3968
Manufactured in the United States of America

In the forest there was a short twig

and a tall tree trunk.

Short, shorter, shortest.

Tall, taller, tallest.

God takes care of all.

In the zoo there was a small baby elephant

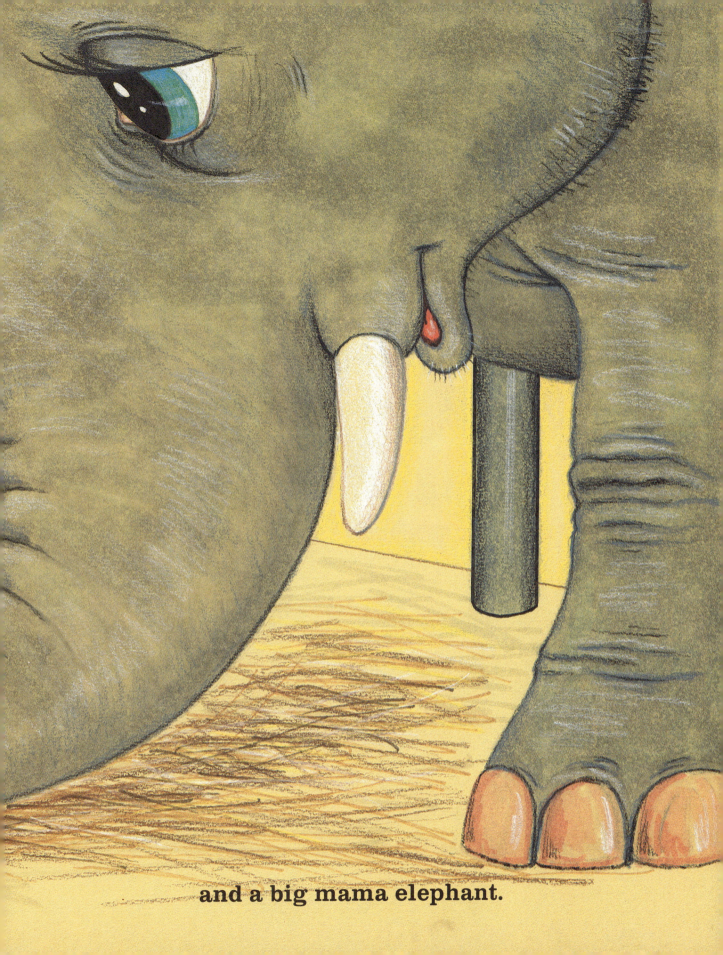

and a big mama elephant.

Small, smaller, smallest.

Big, bigger, biggest.

God takes care of all.

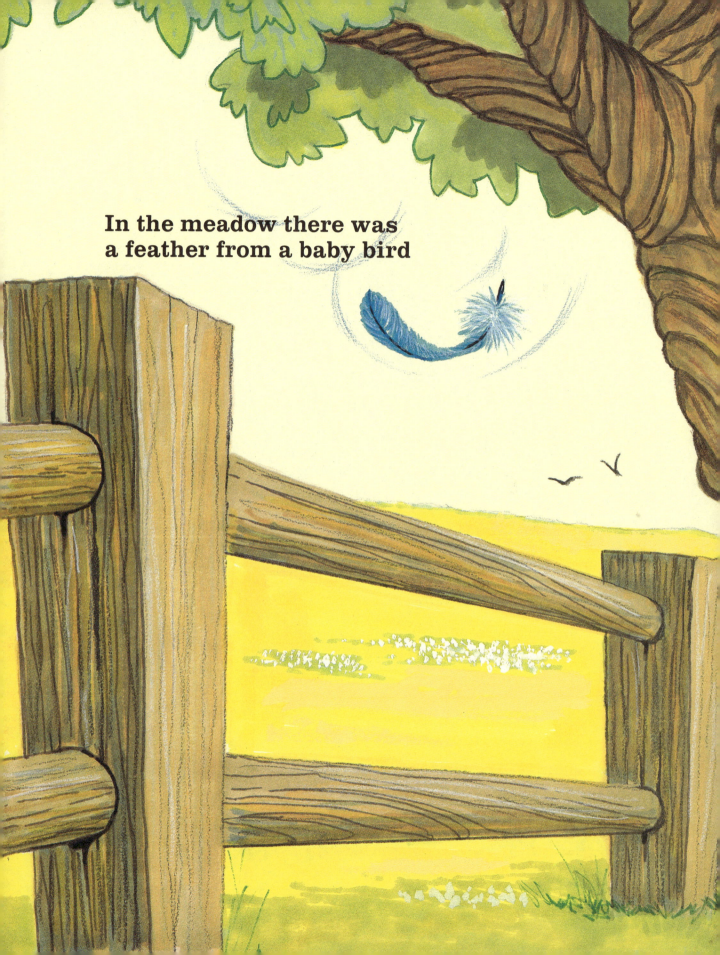

In the meadow there was
a feather from a baby bird

and a heavy nest with a mama bird.

Light, lighter, lightest.

Heavy, heavier, heaviest.

God takes care of all.

**What things are the same?**

# What things are different?

**Same?**

**Different?**

God takes care of all.

Dear family members,

This book will introduce your child to the concept of size. As you read, you will notice that the child is made aware of the contrast in size and then the three words representing the degrees of the sizes. When you read the word, have the child place a finger on the correct size. The book concludes with an opportunity to place the sizes in groups. Again have the child put a finger on the groups which are the same and different. This provides a foundation for later set concepts.

The objects and words also emphasize God's plan for continuation of His creation. Growth progresses from short to tall and small to big. Tell your child that someday he/she will grow up. However, God not only plans for continuation but also for protection of His dear creation. How wonderful is His care and the security your child feels in that care!

Beverly Beckmann